To Gilda and Sammy
with best wishes
from Ian
22.4.83 .

The Trams of Great Britain

in old picture postcards

by
Ian F. Finlay

European Library - Zaltbommel/Netherlands MCMLXXXIII

Cover picture:
An Edwardian card showing this busy junction of five roads in south London. The three double-deck cars are of the open type. The railway bridge across Newington Causeway can be seen in the top left section of the card.

By the same author:
Bachs weltliche Kantaten
A Ladybird Book about Stamp Collecting
A Guide to Foreign-language Printed Patents and Applications
Australian Stamp Collecting
Working with Languages
England off the Beaten Track
Translating (Teach Yourself Books)
Careers in Languages
Language Services in Industry
Post and Postage Stamps (Life French Style)
Which Language Shall I Learn?
The Tram and the Postage Stamp

GB   ISBN 90 288 2144 9

European Library in Zaltbommel/Netherlands publishes among other things the following series:

IN OLD PICTURE POSTCARDS, *a collection in which people can see how a certain place looked like in the Victorian and Edwardian time, which means between 1880 and 1930. It is intended to continue this series and to publish a volume about almost each place in the United Kingdom. In the Netherlands about 1,250 volumes have been published under the title* **In oude ansichten.** *In Germany, Austria and Switzerland respectively 400, 40 and 15 books are edited under the title* **In alten Ansichten;** *in France by the name* **En cartes postales anciennes** *and in Belgium as* **En cartes postales anciennes** *and/or* **In oude prentkaarten** *150 respectively 400 books were published.*

For further particulars about published or forthcoming books, apply to your bookseller or direct to the publisher.

This edition has been printed and bound by Grafisch Bedrijf De Steigerpoort in Zaltbommel/Netherlands.

INTRODUCTION

The beginnings of public transport, as we understand it, in the United Kingdom can probably be said to go back to the first third of the 19th century. There had, of course, for many years prior to then been mail and stage-coaches for conveying post and people from one part of the country to another, while the rich had either their own carriages or used sedan chairs to have themselves carried within cities or towns.

It was, however, the development of the steam engine, largely by George Stephenson, and its use on the railways which may be seen as the beginning of public transport. The first public steam railway in the United Kingdom was that between Stockton and Darlington which opened in September 1825, to be followed just on five years later by the lines from Liverpool to Manchester and from Canterbury to Whitstable in Kent. From these seemingly humble and, to us, certainly primitive beginnings the railways spread, as it were like wild fire, throughout the United Kingdom during the remainder of the 19th century, only to decline again, at least in extent, during the second half of the 20th century.

Whereas the railways, certainly in their earlier years, served mainly to link places beyond city or town limits, there also arose, particularly with the spread of the Industrial Revolution and consequent increase in population of the large cities, the need to convey people within cities and, to a lesser extent, between adjacent or neighbouring centres.

The first means of urban public transport was the horse bus, which made its appearance roughly at the same time as the first railways. While these horse buses clearly served a useful purpose, they had many disadvantages, not the least of which were the cluttering up of the streets and the mess made in them by the horses. Great strain was also put on the vehicles and horses because of the poor road surfaces of the time and the inability of these buses to be used on really steep terrains.

The idea of having bus-like vehicles running on rails, although still pulled by horses, came originally from the United States, the first examples having made their appearance in New York in the early 1830's. The first British tramway of this type was that built in Birkenhead by the American, George Francis Train, in 1860. Because of the relative success of this line, Train moved to London in the following year, where he built three horse tramways, in Bayswater, Westminster and Kennington.

Train's London experiments were however neither

successful nor popular. This was mainly because the rails used projected above the surface of the road and caused great inconvenience to other vehicles as well as being a danger to other road-users. This was not even eliminated entirely by electric tram rails which were laid flush with the road surface, as will be remembered by those who have seen the film 'Genevieve', made in 1953, just after trams had finally disappeared from the streets of London, although not all the track had by then been lifted. There was also the fact that some of Train's tramways had been built in upper- and middle-class districts, the residents of which had their own horse-drawn carriages and, therefore, had no desire or need to use the new means of transport. Throughout the United Kingdom trams were in fact destined to be a working- and lower middle-class form of transport which was used relatively rarely by the upper- and upper-middle classes.

With the development of rails which were flush with the road surface, opposition to the horse tram nevertheless gradually subsided, to the extent that this form of transport spread to most cities and many towns in the United Kingdom during the latter quarter of the 19th century. The horse tram has in fact continued to be used on the Isle of Man to this day, albeit as a summer tourist attraction. In certain cities, particularly on the Continent, the horse tram persisted, in some cases, well into the 20th century. It was in any case the first type of tram to be used on most systems. It nevertheless still possessed most of the disadvantages of the horse bus, although it was easier for the horse(s) to pull cars of greater weight and, therefore, capacity on rails than along the usually poor roads of the time, the resistance offered by friction being less. Double-deck tramcars, a feature common to very many systems in the United Kingdom, were pulled by horses running two abreast. They caused wear to the street not only between the tracks, but also for a distance to both sides of them and, as we shall see later, this also proved inhibiting to the development of electric trams in many cases. Since steam was the form of traction used for the railways, thought was, of course, also given to its use for urban and interurban trams. The first steam trams made their appearance in the United Kingdom in the late 1870's, and this form of traction persisted in certain towns in the Midlands and north of England until the turn of the century. Those who remember steam trains will be aware of their dirtiness from the passengers' point of view. This was also a complaint made about steam trams, added to which they were often also found to frighten the many horses still to be found in the streets. Many ingenious, more or less successful means were developed to reduce these disadvantages of the steam tram, the main one of which was to separate the car housing the engine from the trailer in which the passengers sat. The first steam trams to be built in the United Kingdom nevertheless had a combined engine and car.

Another form of traction used in some cases was a cable. This ran continuously below the road and was gripped by a device passing from the car through a slot in the road. When the device gripped the moving cable, the car, too, was moved. This method of traction was ideal for steep gradients, although its use was not necessarily restricted to them. Cable traction was used on the Highgate Hill tramway in North London from 1884. It was also used at Matlock in Derbyshire from 1893 until 1927, while there was also an extensive and highly complicated cable system in use in Edinburgh for many years. In some cases the gripping mechanism was mounted on a separate car, called the 'dummy', which pulled a trailer in which the passengers sat.

As with the other forms of traction already referred to, many of these trailers had two decks. This was always a typical feature of British trams, although such cars were also to be found in such cities as Barcelona, Copenhagen and Paris, as well as in those in which there was a strong British influence, for example in Hobart in Tasmania, Hong Kong (to this day) and in various cities in South Africa. These two decks had their origin in the influence which the stage-coach exerted on tramway design. Initially the top deck was uncovered, this accounting for the expression 'there's more room outside', which used to be used by some of the older bus conductors in London, since the same applied to the early London double-deck buses.

Bearing in mind that horses and steam were, on the whole, to say the least, inhibiting to the development of trams as a means of urban public transport, there were from the early 1870's many experiments with more esoteric means of traction. They included compressed air, electric batteries, gas and petrol engines. Although the initial results were in some cases quite promising, if not entirely successful for a variety of reasons, most such experiments were short-lived novelties which never really got off the ground or, perhaps more accurately, along the rails.

With the increase in the possibilities of the use of electricity as a form of energy and, more particularly, with the invention of the dynamo by the Belgian Gramme, more and more thought began to be given to the use of this form of energy for trams. The first successful attempt in this direction, albeit it on a small scale, took place in Berlin in 1881, using equipment supplied by Siemens, a firm which is still very active in providing equipment for the most sophisticated of modern electric trams in many parts of the world. There were also many experiments involving electric traction in the United States and Great Britain.

Electrically driven trams gradually made their appearance in the United Kingdom in the early to middle 1890's, although the first electric street tramway had run in Blackpool as early as 1885, and the first electric tramway using an overhead trolley wire in Leeds in 1891. These early electric services were followed by those in Glasgow in 1898 and in Birmingham, London and Manchester in the early years of the 20th century.

The development of the electrically driven tram provided the main impetus for the extension of tramway systems in the United Kingdom. The first decade of the 20th century saw the introduction of systems of greater or lesser extent in almost every city and town of importance, for example Belfast, Derby, Dundee, Gateshead, Leicester, Luton, Swansea and Weston-super-Mare, to mention but a few. Those of such cities as Birmingham, Glasgow, Leeds, London and Manchester were very extensive, not infrequently linking up with those of neighbouring towns, at least when equality of gauge permitted! This latter circumstance gave rise to the interurban tramway, i.e. that linking adjacent towns or cities by running through the villages and countryside separating them, although perhaps not to quite the same extent as the vicinal system in Belgium. There was, for example, a time when it was almost possible to travel from Leeds to Liverpool, via Manchester, solely by changing from one tramway system to another.

Some idea of the extent of the tramway network in Great Britain can be gathered from the figures for 1920, the year in which it reached its peak as far as the number of passengers carried was concerned. In that year 14,258 tramcars carried 4,987 million passengers over 2,729 miles of track, according to Board of Trade returns. As late as 1939 there were still 7,900 trams in Britain, a number which had fallen to 440 by 1960.

Needless to say, the Government and Local Authorities had not allowed all these developments in the way of tramway systems of one type or another to take place unnoticed. The Tramway Act was passed by Parliament in 1870 and was designated as 'an Act to facilitate the construction and to regulate the working of Tramways'. It nevertheless turned out in many ways to be a millstone or albatross around the necks of the many companies building and operating tramways. Amongst the Act's provisions were the obligation of the company operating a tramway to maintain the road between the rails and that extending 18 inches beyond the rails on each side, and the right of the Local Authority through which a tramway passed to purchase the undertaking from the promoters twenty-one years from the time the latter had been empowered to construct it. This latter provision was responsible, at least in part, for the abandonment of certain systems between the Wars. Added to the provisions of the Tramway Act was the disinclination of many Local Authorities to allow overhead wires from which trams could receive their electricity supply, on the grounds that they could be detrimental to the aesthetic appearance of the city or town. Many methods of circumventing this restriction were tried, the use of a slot between the rails for the wheels, through which the car received its electricity supply from below the road via a 'plough' suspended from the car, being the commonest, at least in London. There were in its system several 'change pits' at which the change from conduit to overhead operation and vice versa took place, this frequently giving rise to a large accumulation of motor vehicles behind the halted car.

As has been said, trams were, throughout their history in the United Kingdom, regarded as being a form of transport for the masses. They had quite early acquired a 'cloth cap' image, which was also not to enhance their chances of survival with the rise of the motor bus, trolleybus and private car. On the other hand, the trams had, of course, in many cases made it possible for working people to live in more pleasant surroundings at large distances from their place of work. In some cases they also ran well beyond the limits of towns and cities, thereby offering city-dwellers a welcome opportunity to get away from their normal environment at weekends and on public holidays. Some of the advertisements for trams, for example those running in London, stressed this facility they offered.

Although tramcars had a long life, surprisingly long in many cases, they were expensive to build and, therefore, ultimately to replace. They were, of course, also less flexible than motor buses, in so far as they had to stick to their own track. Some readers may recall the story of the man who had suddenly discovered who he was, namely a person who ran in predestinate grooves. He was, in fact, not even a bus, but a tram! The laying of new track was also expensive, not to mention the resultant disruption to other road-users. Trams were often also the cause of major traffic jams, as witness some of the long queues of them at such busy junctions as the Elephant and Castle in south London. The present roundabout there has even recently been provided with traffic lights.

These were amongst the many reasons which led to the closure of a number of British systems between the Wars; for example, in 1930 in Cheltenham and Peterborough, in 1931 in Carlisle and Scarborough, in 1932 in Accrington and Rochdale, in 1933 in Gloucester and Great Yarmouth, in 1934 in North-hampton and Torquay, in 1935 in Doncaster and York, in 1936 in Dover and Nottingham, in 1937 in Grimsby and Newport, in 1938 in Ashton-under-Lyne and in 1939 in Bath and Halifax. The first complete electric system to be abandoned was that of Sheerness, this having taken place as early as 1917. Many of the major closures took place within the period when a Royal Commission on Transport had, in 1931, condemned tramways. It was in 1935 that London Transport started replacing tramways by trolleybuses, a process which was ultimately to see the running of the last trams in London on 5 July 1952.

Those larger systems which survived World War Two, more or less in their entirety, for example Birmingham, Edinburgh, Glasgow, Leeds, Liverpool, Manchester and Sheffield, had suffered greatly from lack of adequate maintenance during the war years, not to mention the damage to cars, depots and track, as a result of bombing in certain cases. Apart from this, there were also very many more private cars than before the war. There was also still that 'cloth cap' image of the trams which meant that many of them ran through the poorer parts of the cities they served. Also, in London, the only tramway link between parts south and north of the Thames was the Kingsway subway, initially built for single-deck cars, but subsequently enlarged to take double-deck cars which started running through it in January 1931. Bearing in mind that part of this subway is now used by cars, it is perhaps ironic to consider that it presaged a contemporary development in relation to trams in the centre of many continental cities, for example Brussels and Cologne!

Thus it was that even these extensive systems were closed in the 1950's (London in 1952, Birmingham in 1953, Edinburgh in 1956, Liverpool in 1957 and Leeds in 1959) and the early 1960's (Sheffield in 1960 and, last of all, Glasgow on 4 September 1962). Within just over a hundred years of its initial appearance in the United Kingdom the tram had, with the exception of Blackpool and a few museum lines, completely disappeared. Even the Blackpool system has been curtailed over the years, but its future seems assured, if only because of the popularity of that city as a summer tourist resort with its decorated and illuminated tramcars.

Many continental cities, particularly in the Federal Republic of Germany, and those such as Brussels and Amsterdam, have in the post-war years sought to adapt and have been eminently successful in adapting their trams to modern traffic and social conditions. This has been achieved in a variety of ways including, in some cases, placing trams underground in city centres, so that they do not interfere in any way with other road-users. In some cases, Cologne for example, the city tram centre has been integrated with the central railway station. Outside these centres the trams often run on reserved track, enabling high speeds to be reached and sustained for long distances, this being a far cry from, for example, a tram's progress along Amsterdam's Utrechtsestraat! The introduction of ticket-cancelling machines inside cars for tickets purchased in advance from machines at tram stops or at tobacconists has also done away with the need for conductors, meaning that a tram requires merely a driver. The use of articulated vehicles, consisting of three sections, or of a varying number of trailers linked to the motor car, depending on the passenger density, has meant that up to three hundred passengers can be conveyed by one unit operated by one man (or woman) only. This method of operation has not only resulted in a great reduction in labour costs (in countries which also have unions!), but a flat-rate or zonal fare system has also simplified matters considerably, as has a system of fining those without valid tickets on the spot, inspectors in plain clothes, sometimes dressed as hippies, often being employed. This may be considered very un-British, but it is effective, and that is surely what the honest traveller has a right to expect. Various cities in the United Kingdom have come to regret the alacrity with which they abandoned their tramway systems, most of which were, admittedly, at the time of their closure, very much in need of modernisation. Some have in fact commissioned feasibility studies connected with the reintroduction of trams. It must also be conceded that trams are certainly not consumers, at least directly, of what has come to be excessively expensive oil, nor are they major contributors to pollution. A visit to, let us say, Amsterdam, Brussels, Budapest, Munich or Vienna should serve to convince even the most obstinate of the efficacy of an efficient modern tramway system as a highly effective means of late 20th century public transport.

The postcards which follow are all from the writer's collection and have been arranged in alphabetical order of the places in which the trams ran and, within this order, in chronological order of types of traction, i.e. horse, steam, cable and electricity. This arrange-ment means that, in a few cases, trams do not appear under the authority by which they were operated. A few non-specific humorous cars have been placed at the end.

It is fully realized that a selection of a hundred and fifty cards can give merely a very superficial insight into the wide variety of trams once to be seen conveying their passengers along the streets of the United Kingdom. An attempt has however been made to render it as extensive and varied as possible, in the hope that each card will be of specific interest to readers. The brief captions are designed to set the cards more securely in their context.

It should perhaps be mentioned that some cards I should like to have included had to be omitted because of their poor reproducibility. A few such cards have however been included because of their special interest. Each card illustrated is, as it were, a miniature visual aid to interpreting the past, and each has a story to tell in various contexts.

Harrogate, November 1982

S.12288.   CARDIFF STREET, ABERDARE.

1. ABERDARE. This industrial town in South Wales was from just before World War One
until 1935 served by various tram routes which formed part of a fairly extensive network
operating in and around the valleys to the north of Cardiff. This card shows single-deck
car No. 13 in Cardiff Street in Aberdare. The dress of the pedestrians and the lack of
other road transport suggest that the photo was taken during the early years of the
system. Note the transition from double to single track.

Union Street, Aberdeen, looking East

2. ABERDEEN. Amongst the many tramway systems once operating in Scotland that of Aberdeen was an isolated, but progressive example with electric cars running from 1899 until 1955. This card, printed in Germany, shows no fewer than three balcony cars in the city's Union Street. It probably dates from the time of World War One. Note that the drivers are still fully exposed to the elements.

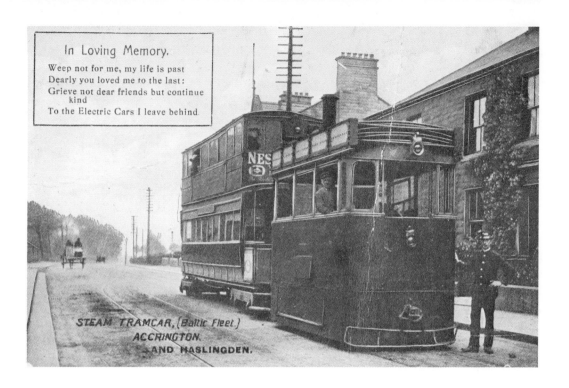

In Loving Memory.

Weep not for me, my life is past
Dearly you loved me to the last:
Grieve not dear friends but continue
    kind
To the Electric Cars I leave behind.

STEAM TRAMCAR, (Baltic Fleet.)
ACCRINGTON.
AND HASLINGDEN.

3. ACCRINGTON. A locally published card issued to mark the replacement by electric cars of the steam trams which ran between Accrington and Haslingden from 1886 to 1907. It shows the typical arrangement of the car housing the engine and the double-deck trailer for the passengers. The driver can be seen leaning out of one of the windows of the engine. A well-known brand of milk is being advertised on the front of the passenger car.

STATION AND STAMFORD NEW ROAD, ALTRINCHAM.

4. ALTRINGHAM. An interesting card showing an open-top car of the Manchester system of which Altringham was a southern outpost. The car is passing the railway station in Stamford New Road and the clock tower. Note the staircase leading to the tram's upper deck and the fact that the driver is still completely exposed to the elements. Such open-top cars were built for Manchester in the early years of the century.

Prestwick Road, Ayr.

5. AYR. Electric trams ran in this Scottish town from 1901 to 1931. Most were of the open-top type, as shown on this card, although there were also enclosed cars and one-man single-deckers. The fact that the card shows two trams in Prestwick Road serves to remind us of the present proximity of Ayr to Prestwick airport. The town was however formerly a popular holiday resort.

Duke Street, Barrow-in-Furness

6. BARROW-IN-FURNESS. The system in this town was an isolated one, in contrast to many others in Lancashire, for example that in and around Manchester. Various types of car were used, that on this card, in the Valentine's series, being of the open-top variety. The system was abandoned in 1932. Note the car's destination board and the interest of those in the street in being photographed.

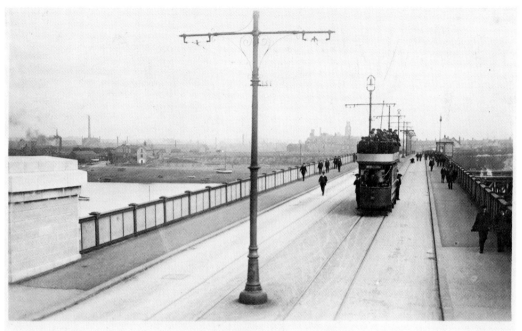

3514   **WALNEY BRIDGE FROM THE PARK.**   SANKEYS.

7. BARROW-IN-FURNESS. A very crowded open-top car on Walney Bridge connecting Barrow with Walney Island which has fine sandy beaches and a nature reserve. Note the elaborate lamp standards in the centre of the road which also support the wires from which the trams obtain their current.

4748.   ZION CHAPEL AND BRANCH AVENUE, BATLEY.

8. BATLEY. Here we have a fine side view of an open-top car in this West Riding wool town to the north-east of Dewsbury. The photo must have been taken on a warm day since all the passengers seem to be riding on the top of the car. Also of interest are the many advertisements on the tram and the distant view of the hills. The card is one in the Kingsway series.

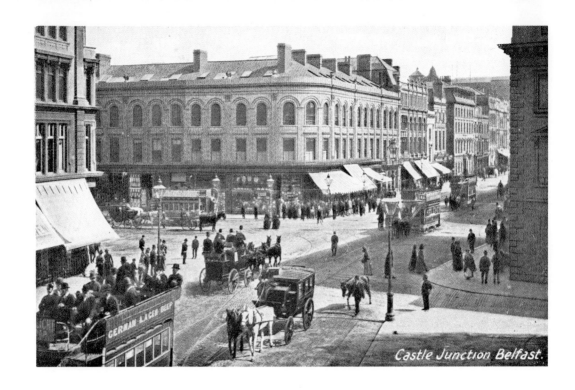

Castle Junction Belfast.

9. BELFAST. The system in this city was the only one of any magnitude in Northern Ireland. The card shows the city's busy Castle Junction. The trams are of the open-top, horse-drawn type. Electrification of the system began in 1905. Note the many other horse-drawn vehicles and the advertisement for German Lager Beep (sic) on the tram in the bottom left.

10. BELFAST. An interesting card in that it shows the same Castle Junction as the former card, but with electric open-top cars. It was posted in August 1906, shortly after electrification of Belfast trams had begun. In contrast to the horse-drawn cars, these electric cars have a railing surrounding the top deck. This city's trams were replaced by trolleybuses from 1938.

11. BELFAST. A view of High Street which is of interest in that it shows the transitional stage between trams, now of the enclosed type, and the trolleybuses which replaced them. The card dates from the late thirties. Note the private cars which were beginning to add to traffic congestion in city centres.

Devonshire Road, Bexhill

Barker's Library, Bexhill-on-Sea

51514

12. BEXHILL-ON-SEA. This card, posted on 20 August 1906, shows a typical open-top electric car of the time. Bexhill, to the west of Hastings, was served by the tramway system which extended for a considerable distance along the south coast. Note the ornate poles, placed between the two sets of rails, for supporting the wires from which the cars received their current. There is also an advertisement for hot cross buns on the window of the shop on the right, suggesting the photo was taken around Easter.

Old Square, Birmingham

Valentines Series

13. BIRMINGHAM. Posted just before Christmas 1903, this card shows the Old Square in the city centre with a fine view of one of the steam trams still running at that time. Note the great similarity in design of the trailer for passengers on this card and that of the first electric cars. This card is yet another in the Valentine's series.

The Lover's Lament

AT THE LOSS OF THE

Old Steam Trams,

Electrocuted Dec. 31st. 1906.

'Twas NOT SWEET OF OLD, as our love we told
On the top of the Old Steam Car,
When a wand'ring breeze, made us cough and sneeze,
With a smell, like rotten eggs and Tar!

But the lights were low, and the pace was slow,
And the corner seats were cosy,
And many a Miss has received a kiss
On the top of the Car
From Perry Barr
Or the Tram that came from Moseley!

Yes, the Electric Car, can go very far,
In a very short space of time
But that dazzling light, is FAR too bright
So each loving pair, have a stony air
Of not being aware, that each other is there
And gone are their joys sublime!

No, the fact that these Cars are painted blue
And are awfully, terribly, painfully new,
And the fact there is plenty of elbow room,
Will never make up for that friendly gloom
And the joys so sweet,
Of the corner seat
ON THE TOP OF THE OLD STEAM CAR.   F.S.R.

SCOTT RUSSELL & CO., B'HAM. SCOTT SERIES.

14. BIRMINGHAM. A commemorative card was issued to mark the change from steam to electricity on the Saltley, Perry Barr, Witton and Lozells trams, the last steam tram running on 31 December 1906. The poem refers to the dirtiness and smell of the steam trams, but praises the opportunity they offered to courting couples in that 'many a Miss has received a kiss on the top of the Car from Perry Barr or the Tram that came from Moseley!'

In Remembrance of

SALTLEY, PERRY BARR, WITTON, & LOZELLS OLD STEAM TRAMS

WHICH STARTED
SERVICE
NOVEMBER 25th,
1884.

PASSING AWAY
OWING
TO AN ELECTRIC
SHOCK
JANUARY 1st, 1907.

"Let not ambition mock their useful toils,
Their homely joys and destiny obscure."

Photo by]

[P. King.

15. BIRMINGHAM. A companion to the previous card, showing one of the steam trams with its driver and conductor. As stated on the card, the steam service started on 25 November 1884 and finished on 31 December 1906 'owing to an electric shock'. The quotation comes from Gray's 'Elegy Written in a Country Churchyard', written in 1750, long before steam trams were even thought of.

Fatal Tram Accident in Birmingham, October 1st, 1907:— 2 KILLED, 17 INJURED.

EDWARDS & CO., Publishers, B'ham.   A. DARK, Printer, 338, Stratford Rd., B'ham.

16. BIRMINGHAM. Trams were not, any more than any other form of public or private transport, immune from accidents, and this card shows the result of one in Birmingham on 1 October 1907 in which two people were killed and seventeen injured. The wrecked double-deck car can be seen on its side with, typically, a huge crowd looking on. The tram's destination had been Edmund Street in the city centre.

BIRMINGHAM CORPORATION TRAMWAYS

LORD MAYOR'S DISTRESS FUND

PLEASE GIVE FREELY

ALL YOU PAY FOR THIS CARD GOES TO THE FUND.

17. BIRMINGHAM. This card shows a lavishly decorated double-deck car and was issued on behalf of Birmingham Corporation Tramways. Proceeds from its sale were to go to the Lord Mayor's Distress Fund. Unfortunately, there is no indication on the card of the reason for the fund. The card nevertheless shows one of the additional uses to which trams were often put in their heyday.

HIGH STREET KINGS HEATH.

325 A

18. BIRMINGHAM. Kings Heath is a district to the south of Birmingham, and this card, posted on 6 September 1917, shows a balcony car on its way from Alcester Lane to Hill Street in the district's High Street. This route was abandoned in October 1949, although Birmingham's last tram ran on 4 July 1953. Note the motor bike and side-car coming along the road on the right. The card was posted to an address in London, and the writer refers to the air raids in that city just before it was sent.

THE GYNN INN, BLACKPOOL.

19. BLACKPOOL. Posted in July 1908, this card is of interest in that it shows one of Blackpool's appropriately named Dreadnought cars together with three more conventional single-deckers of the Blackpool and Fleetwood Tramroad Company. Part of Gynn Inn, a popular meeting-place in Edwardian times, is also visible on the card.

TAKING A TRIP ROUND BLACKPOOL (WHITEGATE DRIVE)

20. BLACKPOOL. A locally produced card, posted in July 1917, showing a completely open single-deck car, with so-called toastrack cross-bench seating, conveying a group of holiday-makers on a circular tour of this popular resort. It is seen in Whitegate Drive, parallel to, but a little inland from the Promenade along the sea front. Note the fine view of the driver standing at his controls.

21. BLACKPOOL. This comic card was posted in July 1924, after the rate for sending postcards had risen from ½d to 1d. It shows an open-top car of the time overflowing with visitors in their blazers and straw hats. It indicates that this resort was no less popular then than it is now with holiday-makers and tourists.

THE ROCKET, BLACKPOOL ILLUMINATIONS

22. BLACKPOOL. Locally produced, this modern card shows one of the many ways in which the resort's trams can be and are decorated and illuminated for use during the height of the tourist season. The fact that it is in the form of a rocket and has representations of satellites on its side indicates that the city has kept up with the times. It is, of course, the only city on the mainland still to have trams as a means of public transport.

The Square, Bournemouth.

23. BOURNEMOUTH. A view of the Square in this popular south-coast resort with an open-top car on its way to Christchurch at the eastern outpost of the Bournemouth system. The conductor can be seen leaning against the rear platform of the car. In common with many cards from seaside resorts, there seem to be more passengers on the top of the car than inside it. The card was posted in April 1914.

Sachs, Bradford (Copyright).

BRADFORD TRAM ACCIDENT, July 31st, 1907.

24. BRADFORD. 1907 seems to have been a bad year for tram accidents (cf. No. 16). This one occurred on 31 July of that year in this well-known Yorkshire city. The card shows the top section of the car on the left and its lower section on the right. The area affected has been cordoned off, and there are several policemen in attendance.

TOWN HALL, BRADFORD.

25. BRADFORD. This view of two open-top cars in front of Bradford's imposing town hall is of interest in that the driver and conductor of the front car can be seen posing by its side. The complicated track lay-out can also be seen, indicating that Town Hall Square was one of the main and busiest centres for trams in the city's extensive network which was finally abandoned in 1950.

Town Hall Square, Bradford

Yuletide Greetings.

26. BRADFORD. A very similar view of Town Hall Square to that on the previous card. Bearing in mind that there are several people on the top of the tram, it seems likely that the snow was added to the card to create a yuletide atmosphere. Trams were however, in general, capable of coping with snow very much better than most other types of road vehicle.

North Gate, Royal Pavilion, Brighton

Valentines Series   39501

27. BRIGHTON. An attractive card showing an open-top car on its way to Queen's Park Road passing the North Gate of the city's Royal Pavilion, built in oriental style by John Nash for the Prince Regent. Brighton's trams ran until August 1939. The system was in some ways unique in that most of its trams were built in the department's own workshops.

Bristol Tramways. Illuminated Car.
December, 1925.

28. BRISTOL. Standing outside a depot, this special illuminated car has been made to resemble Noah's ark, and a variety of small animals can be seen at the windows along its side. In common with the Birmingham car (No. 17), it is also drawing attention to the Lord Mayor's Fund, in this case specified as being for children's Christmas dinners. The card is dated December 1925.

Tramway Centre, Bristol.

29. BRISTOL. The city's Tramway Centre was a favourite subject for Bristol cards. This example shows no fewer than five trams of various designs, but all with open tops. Bristol abandoned its trams in 1941, and the presence of a motor bus on the card was an ominous sign. Note the advertisement for Grace Moore, a well-known actress and singer of the thirties outside the Hippodrome on the left and the cathedral behind it.

Electric Tram Station, Bushmills

30. BUSHMILLS. A view of the electric tram station at this town in Antrim in Northern Ireland. The line, just under nine miles in length, ran to Portrush. There was also a line from Bushmills to the Giant's Causeway. Both lines opened in the 1880's, and some of the Bushmills lines survived to the late 1940's. This card was posted in July 1914. Everyone present obviously wanted to be in the photo.

31. CAMBRIDGE. This university city had a small network of horse trams from 1880 until 1914. The system was never electrified and used both single-deck and open-top cars. This comic card, posted in May 1905, gives the impression that the system was already on its last legs in 1905, to judge from the dozing conductor at the back and the one female passenger inside the mended car. Even the horse looks emaciated and has a plaster on its back.

Clarence Bridge, Cardiff.

32. CARDIFF. This Welsh city had an efficient tramway system which was not finally abandoned until early in 1950. This card shows an open-top car passing over Clarence bridge across the river Taff. It was opened in 1890 and was then the largest swinging road bridge in the country. The taking of this photo was obviously a major event for the locals. Note the sign on the lamp-standard 'All Cars Stop Here'.

Queen Street and Dominion Buildings, Cardiff

33. CARDIFF. An enclosed car in Queen Street in the centre of Cardiff. Some very well-known names can be seen on the buildings on the left, and no-one could fail to locate the establishment of Hugh Owen, dentist, on the right! Cardiff's Queen Street is now a pedestrian precinct.

English Street. Carlisle.

34. CARLISLE. The system in this city has been described as the most isolated in Great Britain, being fifty miles or so from any other. The card shows English Street as it was in about 1907 with an open-top car on its way to Newtown, one of the termini of the system. The Lonsdale statue was erected in August 1847. Carlisle trams were replaced by buses in 1931, having been preceded by horse buses from 1896 to 1900.

PITTVILLE GATES, CHELTENHAM.

BURROW'S BRITISH COLOUR SERIES, CHELTENHAM

35. CHELTENHAM. An attractive card which shows the entrance to Pittville Park in the northern part of Cheltenham. This was another example of an isolated system. The card shows two open-top cars, and the whole scene evokes the rather relaxed atmosphere of an Edwardian spa. The city's trams were replaced by buses in 1930.

Chester, Eastgate Street

36. CHESTER. A fine view of an open-top car in Eastgate Street, the city's main thoroughfare, which has different names for its various sections. Note the half-timbered houses so characteristic of the city centre. Chester trams were replaced by buses in 1930. The card was printed in Germany, as were very many showing British scenes in the years prior to World War One.

The Chatsworth Road Tram Terminus. Chesterfield.

37. CHESTERFIELD. A very obviously posed, but excellent view of an open-top car at the Chatsworth Road terminus, the main road out of the city to Buxton and Bakewell. What a pleasant change to see a tram in relatively rural surroundings! The city's electric trams ran from December 1904 until March 1927. Car No. 7, seen here, was amongst the first batch, built in 1904. The card was postally used in July 1905.

Tramway Terminus, Chingford.

38. CHINGFORD. Situated at the north-eastern extremity of Epping Forest, Chingford —
although in Essex — might well be considered as being in the greater London area. There
is definitely a rural appearance about this early open-top electric car and its surroundings.
One begins to wonder whether the photo was taken for the sake of the tram, the public
house or the covered cart with its two horses waiting patiently. At its peak, the tramway
network in outer North London extended into Middlesex, Essex and Hertfordshire.

NORTH HILL, COLCHESTER.

39. COLCHESTER. North Hill, part of which is shown on this card, was too steep for horse trams. A steam tram route planned for it never materialised, and electric trams started operating on it in 1904, these continuing until 1929 when they were replaced by motor buses. Some idea of the steepness of the hill can be gained from this view of an open-top car making its way up the 1 in 12 gradient. Note the ornate post supporting the overhead wires for the tram.

BROADGATE. COVENTRY.

40. COVENTRY. Two open-top cars in Broadgate in the centre of Coventry, whose trams were electrified as early as 1895. Abandonment of part of the system took place in 1936-37, but final closure did not occur until the autumn of 1940, after the disastrous air raid on the city. The card was printed in Germany, in this case for a Birmingham publisher.

NORTHERN ECHO SNAPSHOT.

FIRST CAR DRIVEN BY THE MAYORESS
(MRS. A. HENDERSON).

41. DARLINGTON. Posted in July 1904, this card was issued to mark the opening of Darlington Corporation Light Railways on 1 June 1904. It shows the first car being driven by the then Mayoress, Mrs. A. Henderson. The city's first cars were single-deckers, double-deckers being added later in the system's history. Darlington trams were replaced by trolleybuses in 1926.

42. DARLINGTON. Single-deck cars were still running when this card was posted in July 1912. The car, No. 4 of the first series of sixteen, is proceeding along Northgate, in the city centre, on its way to the Market Place. Note the fine horse-drawn carriage with its driver wearing a top hat.

London Road, Derby

43. DERBY. Electric trams ran in this city from 1904 until 1934. This early Edwardian card shows one of the first batch of open-top cars with which the system opened. It is seen in London Road on its way to Midland Railway station. One wonders what the boys are doing squatting at the base of the pole supporting the overhead wires.

1.140. Leaving the Course. Doncaster

44. DONCASTER. An interesting card which shows two balcony cars, built in 1913, waiting to take the crowds leaving the city's race course back to the city centre. This was not the only form of transport, as the many horse-drawn vehicles and occasional motor car show. Doncaster's electric tram system was in operation from 1902 until 1935. Unlike many others in Yorkshire, it was an isolated system, one of its termini being at the race course.

16096 KING STREET & G. P. O.　　　　DOVER.

45. DOVER. This card, posted in January 1905, shows an open-top car in the city's King Street with, on the right, the General Post Office. Note the elaborate pole, surmounted by a lamp, supporting the overhead wires for the trams. Dover's tram system was a fairly small and isolated one, which was replaced by buses on 1 January 1937.

46. DUNDEE. The centre of the British jute industry, this city had electric trams from 1900 until 1956 and was, therefore, amongst the last of the British systems to be abandoned, although those in Edinburgh, Aberdeen and Glasgow outlived it. This card shows two enclosed and one balcony car in the city's High Street in about 1930. Note the complicated track lay-out and the occasional private motor car.

47. EDINBURGH. Princes Street in Scotland's capital has had more than its fair share of postcards devoted to it. This one, posted in August 1912, shows the street at the time when open-top cable trams with a characteristic seating arrangement were still in use. The slot between the rails for lowering the device to grip the moving cable can be seen on the card. Edinburgh's last cable tram ran as late as 1923.

EDB 35   PRINCES STREET, EDINBURGH   A TUCK CARD

48. EDINBURGH. Produced by the well-known firm of Raphael Tuck & Sons Ltd., this card shows a very much later view of Princes Street. The trams are now all of the enclosed electric type, and there is also a double-decker bus. It is virtually impossible to count the number of trams making their way in one direction or another along this famous street. Edinburgh's last tram ran on 16 November 1956.

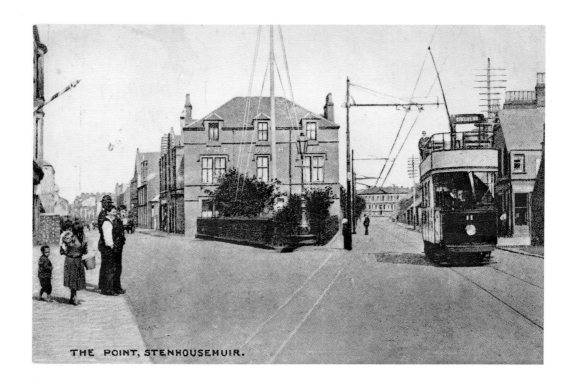

THE POINT, STENHOUSEMUIR.

49. FALKIRK. Some twenty-five miles to the west of Edinburgh, this industrial town had a fairly compact system of electric trams from October 1905 until July 1936. The system was a circular one connecting Falkirk and Larbert, where this card was posted in October 1909, with the Carron Ironworks. Stenhousemuir was also on this route, and the card shows car No. 11 passing the Plough Hotel there on its circular route.

BAINSFORD BRIDGE
FALKIRK

50. FALKIRK. This city's circular tramway system was also of interest in that its seven miles involved crossing no fewer than ten bridges, including two swing bridges over a canal. This card, posted in October 1910, shows one of the system's open-top cars crossing Bainsford bridge. Judging by the number of onlookers, it was obviously an interesting event.

51. GATESHEAD. A fine view of two Newcastle Corporation cars (Nos. 225 and 213), dating from 1915 and 1914 respectively. When equality of gauge and proximity permitted, it quite often happened that cars from different cities used the same track for at least part of their routes. Gateshead's own electric trams ran from 1901 until 1951, as did those of Newcastle. This card was postally used in February 1943.

52. GLASGOW. This city had one of the longest reigns of electric trams in the United Kingdom, i.e. from 1898 until 1 September 1962, although some lines began to be abandoned from 1948. This card shows two balcony cars in Union Street in the city centre. Judging from the number of passengers entering and leaving them, there is little doubt that the system was well used. Even before World War Two Glasgow had possibly the best trams in Europe, the so-called 'Coronations'.

The Cross, Gloucester.

53. GLOUCESTER. This city's system was never a very large one, having merely thirty cars during its heyday. It was replaced by buses between 1927 and 1933. There had once been proposals to link up with Cheltenham via through connexions, but these were never realized. This card shows a crowded open-top car in the fairly narrow and busy Cross in the centre of the city.

Gt. Yarmouth. Arrival of London Boat.

54. GREAT YARMOUTH. Norfolk's popular holiday resort had electric trams from 1902 until 1933. This interesting card shows two different types of open-top cars on the quay at the time of the arrival of a paddle steamer from London. The card was posted in September 1904 and shows Great Yarmouth's first batch of cars, built in 1902. Note the windmills on the other side of the river Yare.

GUERNSEY. QUAY, St. PETER PORT.

55. GUERNSEY. The quay at St. Peter Port where the line, previously operated by steam, was electrified as early as 1892 and continued to run between St. Peter Port and St. Sampsons until 1934. The majority of the cars was of the open-top type, as on the card, although there were also some trailers, a relatively rare phenomenon in the United Kingdom. Note the advertisement for 'Zebra' grate polish on the front of the tram.

TRAM ACCIDENT AT HALIFAX.

SUNDAY, JULY 1ST 1906.

56. HALIFAX. Possibly the main feature of the Yorkshire tram system was its multiplicity of gauges, this being a major handicap to expansion and through running. Halifax, for example, had the narrow 3 ft. 6 in. This card shows open-top car No. 94 on its side, as a result of an accident on Sunday, 1 July 1906. The shortness of the wheelbase and narrowness of gauge are very apparent.

21964   STUMP CROSS, HALIFAX.

57. HALIFAX. Most of the cards previously featured have shown trams in more or less congested city centres, even if at a time when there was considerably less traffic than today. This card, posted in July 1913, shows car No. 87 of the Halifax system on the route to Brighouse approaching the junction at Stump Cross, well beyond the confines of the city centre.

Cadzow Street, Hamilton

58. HAMILTON. In common with Yorkshire, there was a wide variety of gauges in use for trams in Scotland, the Hamilton system having the rather unusual 4 ft. 7¾ in. This card, posted in May 1911, shows an open-top car in the city's Cadzow Street. Hamilton gained notoriety in May 1941 when Rudolf Hess landed on the estate of the local duke.

59. HASTINGS. This popular resort was amongst the many places on the south and
south-east coast formerly to have trams. Because of objections to overhead wires, sections
of the Hastings system, including that shown on the card, had a surface-contact system
for collecting current. This well-filled open-top car is on its way to Hastings Memorial.
The system also ran to Bexhill-on-Sea (cf. No. 12).

ANLABY ROAD, HULL.

60. HULL. The City of Hull Tramways operated from 1899 until 1945 and therefore had a considerably longer life than many other British systems. This card, posted in 1927, shows a balcony car in Anlaby Road, one of the main thoroughfares leading to the city centre. Note the centre groove rail typical of the system and the fact that routes were identified by letters rather than numbers.

High Street, Ilford

61. ILFORD. Over the years very many systems operated in what we should perhaps today consider to be the greater London area. Because of uniformity of gauge, it was possible for the lines of one undertaking to link up with those of another. This card, posted just before the outbreak of World War One, shows a balcony car in High Street on its way to Goodmayes. Ilford cars connected at appropriate points with those of Barking and East Ham in the eastern part of London.

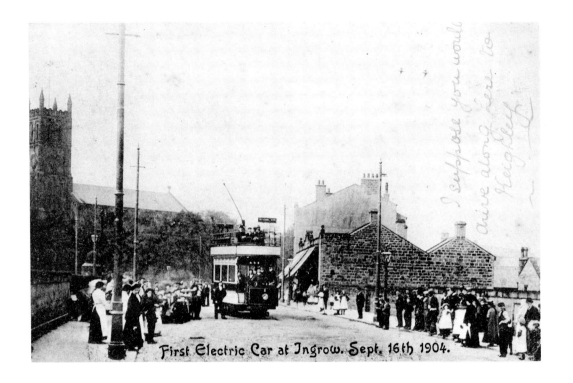

First Electric Car at Ingrow. Sept. 16th 1904.

62. INGROW. The inauguration of the first electric car was a major event in any community, to be marked, in the case of Ingrow in Yorkshire, part of the system of Keighley Corporation, by the issuing of a postcard showing not only the car, but also most of the local population. Various dignitaries also appear to be riding on the open-top car. The event took place on 16 September 1904, and the card was posted later in that same year.

THE ELECTRIC POWER STATION. IPSWICH.

63. **IPSWICH.** An interesting picture of an open-top electric tram at Constantine Road depot in about 1904, shortly after operation started in November 1903. The electric power station can be seen behind the depot. It should not be forgotten that local tram and electricity companies were often formally connected commercially. The depot is a typical example of early tramway architecture. The last trams ran in Ipswich in 1926, a relatively early closing date.

Cornhill and Tavern Street, Ipswich

64. IPSWICH. Three Ipswich Corporation Tramways' cars at Cornhill in the centre of the city during the early years of the system's operation. Note the complicated track lay-out at the busy junction. Of interest is also the profusion of horse-drawn vehicles and the lone early motor car by the memorial.

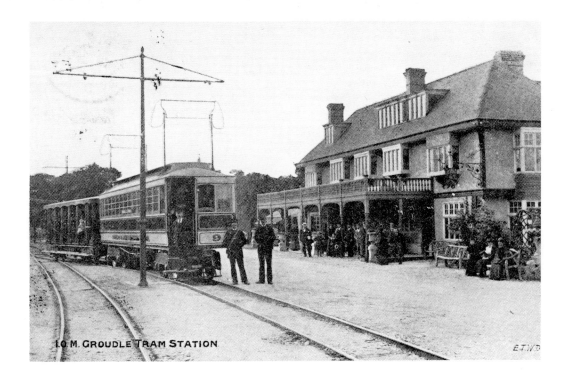

I.O.M. GROUDLE TRAM STATION

E.T.W.D

65. ISLE OF MAN. The eastern section of the island had many tramways over the years. This card, posted at Douglas in August 1905, shows the tram station at Groundle Glen on what is known as the Manx Electric Railway. Standing at the station is a single-deck motor car and an open-sided trailer. The railway ran from Derby Castle to Ramsey, much of the line being on reserved track.

66. ISLE OF MAN. The Snaefell Mountain Railway runs from Laxey to Snaefell Summit at a height of 2,034 feet. Here, one of the cars, inscribed Snaefell Mountain Tramway, is en route to the summit. The length of the line is 4.62 miles. Electric power is received from bows of unusual design at each end of the car. There is a supplementary centre rail to prevent derailment and assist braking on the downward journey. This is another example of a card printed in Germany.

OXFORD STREET, KIDDERMINSTER.

67. **KIDDERMINSTER**. An attractive card, posted in October 1906, showing car No. 3 of the Kidderminster and Stourport Electric Tramway Company in Oxford Street. The system operated from 1898 until 1929. These cars were also used with trailers, a fairly uncommon practice in the United Kingdom, although quite common on the Continent.

High Street, Kirkcaldy

68. KIRKALDY. A fine view of an open-top car in the High Street of this port and industrial town on the Firth of Forth, which was also the birthplace of Adam Smith of 'The Wealth of Nations' fame. The car is on a single track section, not surprisingly bearing in mind the narrowness of the street. Kirkaldy trams ran from 1903 until 1931 and had the narrow gauge of 3 ft. 6 in. The card was posted in November 1913.

The Last Car from Leeds

69. LEEDS. This comic card, posted in March 1907, was drawn by 'Cynicus', the pseudonym of Martin Anderson (1854-1932). A Scot by birth, he eventually set up his own company at Tayport in Fife. The company produced many cards referring to aspects of Edwardian life. This particular design also turns up in relation to cities other than Leeds. As the writer of the card says: 'Hope you will never have to do this.'

WELCOME TO OUR KING & QUEEN

ILLUMINATED ELECTRIC CAR.
King's Visit, July 7th, 1908. There are 3000 Electric Lights & requires 150 Horse Power to run it.

70. LEEDS. A locally produced card showing an illuminated Leeds car, specially decorated for a visit by Edward VII and Queen Alexandra to the city on 7 July 1908. The 'A.R.' on the side of the car stands for 'Alexandra Regina'. It is stated on the card that there were three thousand electric lights on the car and that one hundred and fifty horse power were required to run it.

The Old Oak, Headingley, Leeds.

71. LEEDS. The majority of cards from large cities tend to show their centres. It is therefore a pleasant change to find subjects of a more rural character. This card, postally used in March 1928, shows a road in Headingley, a northern suburb of Leeds, famous for its cricket-ground. Open-top car No. 164 can be seen passing the preserved remains of a large oak tree.

BOAR LANE, LEEDS. 560/38.

72. LEEDS. This city had an extensive tramway network, and some of its cars were ultimately amongst the most modern in the country. This card shows three double-deck cars of different designs in busy Boar Lane in the city centre. Car No. 171, at the rear on the right, still has an open top. The last trams ran in Leeds on 7 November 1959, on the route from Crossgates to Temple Newsam, a stately home. This card was posted in September 1917.

London Road, Leicester

73. LEICESTER. A delightful card which shows a Leicester Corporation open-top car in London Road, which runs in a south-easterly direction out of the city centre from London Road station. Its destination is Clarendon Park. Electric trams ran in Leicester from 1904 until 1949, and the card shows car No. 27, one of the batch built in the first year of their running.

74. LEICESTER. This comic card, produced in the very early days of the city's electric trams, gives some idea of the number of cars at the junction of several roads dominated by Leicester's best-known edifice, the Victorian Clock Tower which incorporates statues of Simon de Montfort and other city benefactors. The writer of the card, posted in September 1904, suggests that 'the very 'old man' himself would have to worry here'.

75. LEICESTER. A further comic card from this city, bearing all manner of advice to intending passengers. It is representative of the many comic cards which were produced during the early days of electric trams. Similar cards accompanied the early days of bicycles and motor cars.

HUMBERSTONE GATE, LEICESTER.   110.

76. LEICESTER. A relatively late card shows car No. 84, originally built as an open-top type in 1904, but rebuilt in enclosed form between 1924 and 1934. It is running along Humberstone Gate which leads to the junction at the Clock Tower (cf. No. 74). Note the complicated track lay-out and the road number A 47 on the post on the left.

77. LITTLEBOROUGH. This comic card, posted in July 1912, draws attention to one of the pleasures to be derived from riding on the top of an open car (cf. No. 14). Littleborough ultimately became part of the Rochdale system. There was a dense tramway network in that part of Lancashire. Rochdale trams had through services to Bury and Oldham.

LIME STREET, L. & N. W. HOTEL.   LIVERPOOL.

A contribution to your collection.

G.

1292

78. **LIVERPOOL.** This, the earliest card in the book, is of the undivided back type, i.e. that in which the address only was to be written on the reverse, there being a small space for the message on the obverse. It shows a variety of horse-drawn trams in Lime Street with the L. & N.W. hotel. Part of St. George's Hall can be seen on the left. The card was posted on 11 March 1901 and was cancelled by a stamp bearing Queen Victoria's head.

Lord Street   Liverpool

79. **LIVERPOOL**. Three types of electric cars in busy Lord Street in the city centre. Car No. 454, on the left, is a balcony type, No. 394 on the right is an open-top type, while there is a single-decker behind No. 454. Liverpool's horse trams (cf. No. 78) were replaced by electric cars between 1898 and 1901. This card was printed in Germany and posted in July 1904.

Liverpool from the Landing Stage   Valentines Series

80. LIVERPOOL. Here we see three trams, two open-top and one balcony. The view has been taken from the Landing Stage with its dock area along the Mersey river on the other side of which are Wallasey and Birkenhead and the popular Wirral resort of New Brighton (cf. No. 109). It is near the site of the present tunnels under the Mersey.

Liverpool from the Landing Stage

81. **LIVERPOOL.** Exactly the same view as the previous one, except that everything has been given a covering of snow (cf. No. 26). This is a comparatively mild example of what could be done to a card by a publisher. There are cases in which trams or other vehicles have been added or removed or even a more modern type of tram substituted for an older one, in an attempt to produce another picture for the public to purchase.

G.902. CHURCH STREET, LIVERPOOL.

82. LIVERPOOL. This comparatively late card shows a host of trams in the city's Church Street. The two cars in the foreground are of a very modern type. The Liverpool tramway system finally closed on 14 September 1957, many of its so-called 'Green Goddess' cars having been sold to Glasgow between 1953 and 1954. The traffic congestion caused by trams is evident from this card.

TRAM ASCENDING THE GREAT ORME, LLANDUDNO.

83. LLANDUDNO. Posted in July 1939, this picturesque card shows car No. 5 ascending to the summit of the Great Orme's Head overlooking this popular North Wales resort. These cars still run in the summer season. Traction is by cable, the overhead wire being used for signalling purposes only. The line was opened in the early years of the century. The maximum gradient is 1 in 3.6, and the line climbs six hundred feet in little more than a mile.

HIGHBURY. — Upper Street.

84. LONDON. This huge and heterogeneous city was by no means the first in the country to electrify its trams. It was not in fact until July 1901 that the first public electric line opened in north London. There were therefore still many horse trams at the beginning of the postcard era. This card, posted in November 1903, shows an open-top horse car in Upper Street in North London, on the route between Highgate and Moorgate.

Arsenal Gates.   *Woolwich.*

85. LONDON. On a card, posted in March 1906, three open-top horse-drawn trams are seen outside the gate of Woolwich Arsenal in south-east London. Each of these cars is being pulled by two horses. The London County Council had in 1905 purchased the Woolwich & South-East London Tramways, this company until then having operated horse trams on a private basis.

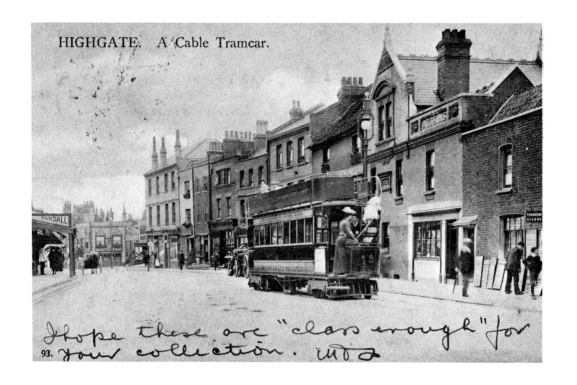

HIGHGATE. A Cable Tramcar.

I hope these are "class enough" for your collection. MB

93.

86. LONDON. Cable traction offered special advantages on hilly routes. There was one such system in North London, from Archway Tavern to Highgate. This card, posted in July 1904, shows one of the open-top cars used on this route. It closed in August 1909, and another cable line, from Kennington Park to Streatham Hill in South London, was converted to electric conduit traction in the same year.

T.R.H THE PRINCE & PRINCESS OF WALES
INAUGURATING THE L.C.C. ELECTRIC TRAMS, MAY 15TH 1903.

87. LONDON. A commemorative card, posted in August 1903, shows the inauguration of the first London County Council electric trams on 15 May of that year by the then Prince and Princess of Wales, the future King George V and Queen Mary. The Prince drove the inaugural car, painted white, for part of the journey to Tooting. The route ran from Westminster Bridge to Tooting via Kennington Road, Clapham and Balham. Note the lack of overhead wires for aesthetic reasons and the use of a central slot for the 'plough'.

88. LONDON. Single-deck trams were, apart from service cars, the exception rather than the rule in the United Kingdom, even from the earliest days of electric trams. Here is an exception which ran on the so-called Alexandra Palace Electric Railway in North London from the early years of the century until the 1930's. The line was operated by Metropolitan Electric Tramways. The Palace, built in 1873, can be seen in the background.

Tram Terminus.

89. LONDON. Crystal Palace in South London was also served by electric trams, and this fine card shows an open-top car of the South Metropolitan Electric Tramways and Lighting Company Ltd. at its terminus outside the Palace. As can be seen, the car received its power from an overhead wire, a method forbidden in many parts of London for aesthetic reasons (cf. No. 87). The Palace, built in 1852, was destroyed by fire in 1936.

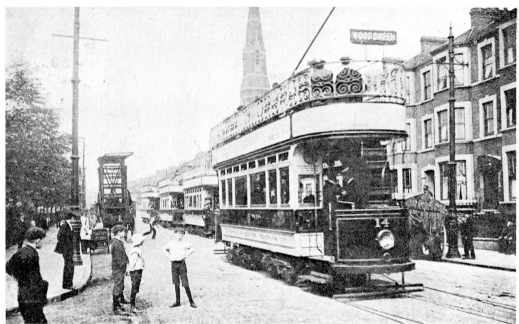

New Electric Trams at Finsbury Park.

90. LONDON. This card, posted in August 1904, shows a line of four new electric open-top cars at Finsbury Park in Seven Sisters Road, waiting to start their journey to Wood Green. This line was operated by Metropolitan Electric Tramways, as were many of the routes in North London. Note the elaborate grating enclosing the top deck and the horse-drawn overhead maintenance vehicle on the left.

2. High Street. Barnet.

91. LONDON. Barnet church, at the top of the hill in High Street, about twelve miles north of Central London, was the terminus of an electric line operated by Metropolitan Electric Tramways Company. This line initially ran to Highgate, but was extended in the 1930's to Moorgate. This card was posted in November 1909 and shows car No. 116 in its original open-top condition. It evokes a charming impression of late-Edwardian suburban life.

277 LONDON. — *Westminster Bridge.* —

92. **LONDON.** Enclosed car No. 320 on Westminster Bridge with an open-top car following it. Note the slot between the rails for obtaining current, overhead wires not being permitted in the inner parts of London for aesthetic reasons. Big Ben and the Houses of Parliament can be seen in the background. The card was posted in August 1910.

812   CLAPHAM. – High Street. –

93. LONDON. A card, posted in September 1907, and featuring an open-top car passing along High Street, Clapham in south-west London. Note the station of the City and South London Electric Railway, described as the quickest route to the West End. There is plenty of activity in the picture with a wide variety of other vehicles, pedestrians and shops.

UXBRIDGE, EALING & SHEPHERDS BUSH ELECTRIC TRAMWAYS. (COPYRIGHT). *"Wakefield" Series. Ealing, W.* No. 113

94. LONDON. A long procession of decorated open-top cars of Uxbridge, Ealing & Shepherds Bush Electric Tramways. The event was occasioned by a visit by Edward VII. The destination of the front car is Southall on the route to Uxbridge to the west of London. Note that these cars receive their electricity supply from overhead wires, not by the conduit system used nearer the centre of the city. The card was posted in October 1906.

Camberwell Green from S.W. No. 3

95. LONDON. Printed in Saxony, this card presents a fine view of open-top car No. 206 on its way to Blackfriars Bridge. Although taken by a local photographer, it depicts a kaleidoscopic view of the 'street life' of the time. Camberwell Green is still a busy centre for a number of bus routes in south-west London.

651

Published by P. S. & V., Lewisham

Nelson Street, Greenwich

96. LONDON. An open-top car in Nelson Street, Greenwich, in south-east London, with a fine view of Greenwich church in the background. In common with the car on the previous card, this tram's destination is also Blackfriars Bridge. Once again, the card presents a lively impression of the 'street life' of the time. Note the variety of goods outside the corner shop on the left and its sign 'Money lent to any amount'.

LONDON, ST. THOMAS'S HOSPITAL AND WESTMINSTER BRIDGE.

97. LONDON. Presenting a panoramic view of Westminster Bridge and St. Thomas's Hospital, this card is of interest in that it shows both double-deck and single-deck cars. The latter were used on the routes connecting South and North London via the Kingsway subway which was completed in April 1908. It was later enlarged to take double-deck cars. More than ten trams can be seen on this card, which gives some idea of the density of tram traffic in Edwardian London.

98. LONDON. A single-decker emerges from the north end of Kingsway subway, about to turn into Theobalds Road on its way to the Angel at Islington. The driver has seemingly forgotten to change the tram's destination which still reads 'Kennington', the southern terminus of the route. The card, sold for 1d, was issued in connexion with a St. Paul's Hospital competition and states that it would be possible to win '£1000 for 1d'.

Thames Embankment and New Scotland Yard London

99. LONDON. This late Edwardian card shows enclosed car No. 461 passing along the Embankment outside New Scotland Yard, with a view of Big Ben and the Houses of Parliament in the background. It has just passed on open-top car about to cross Westminster Bridge on its way to South London. The conduit for current collection can be seen between the rails on the left. The Embankment was one of the busiest tram thoroughfares in London.

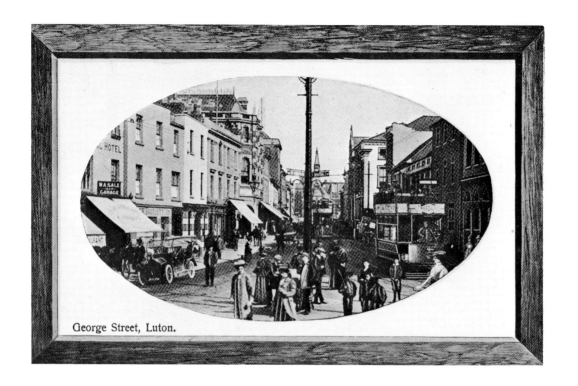

George Street, Luton.

100. LUTON. A system of electric trams operated here from 1908 until 1932, when they were replaced by motor buses. This card, posted in January 1915, shows two of the system's twelve open double-deck cars in George Street in the city centre. The system was an isolated one and is a good example of a relatively small city having its own trams during the heyday of this form of urban public transport.

CHEETHAM HILL VILLAGE.

101. MANCHESTER. Posted in July 1905, this card shows an open-top car in Cheetham Hill village, at the north-western part of the extensive Manchester system. It is a very good example of the photographer obviously being unable to do his work without attracting the attention of most of the local inhabitants. The card is addressed to 'The Mrs of the House'!

ROYAL INFIRMARY AND ESPLANADE, MANCHESTER

102. MANCHESTER. An interesting card, not merely because of the large number of crowded open-top cars, but also since it is made of aluminium. Such cards had to be sent under cover, i.e. in an envelope. They therefore attracted the letter rate of postage. The card shows the city's Royal Infirmary with a fine view of the wide Esplanade.

Deansgate, Manchester

103. MANCHESTER. Open-top car No. 395, one of the batch built between 1901 and 1903, making its way along a fairly deserted Deansgate, one of the city's main thoroughfares. Manchester had an extensive tramway system, radiating in three directions from the city centre, being bordered on the west by that of Salford (cf. No. 127). The system was abandoned between 1946 and 1949, the last car running on 9 January of that year.

V 266-3 MANCHESTER DEANSGATE RAPID PHOTO E C

104. MANCHESTER. Another view of Deansgate with a line of five open-top cars, the first of which, No. 52, has the destination Swinton. Note that the driver is still fully exposed to the elements, making his job not the pleasantest in bad weather. Throughout its history of about fifty years the Manchester system had well over a thousand cars of various types.

38149 The Fort, Margate. J.V.

105. MARGATE. This popular Kent resort and former port was served by a line run by the Isle of Thanet Electric Supply Co. Ltd., which also served Westbrook, St. Peters, Broadstairs and Ramsgate (cf. No. 124). The line was replaced by buses in 1937. Here a crowded open-top car together with three highly decorated floats is seen passing along the sea front. Note the bandstand and the pier in the background.

106. MATLOCK. A view of Crown Square in this popular Derbyshire resort with one of the three open-top cars used to operate the cable tramway up Matlock Bank. The route, 0.62 mile in length, had a maximum gradient of 1 in 5½ and was claimed to be the steepest street tramway in the world. It was the gift of Sir George Newnes and ran until 1927, when it was replaced by buses using a less steep route.

CLOCK TOWER & CENTRAL PROMENADE, MORECAMBE

107. MORECAMBE. This popular Lancashire resort enjoyed the distinction of having the last horse-drawn trams on the mainland. They were not replaced by buses until 1926. Posted in September 1915, this card shows several open-top horse-drawn cars passing along the Central Promenade on Morecambe Bay. To judge from the crowds and general activity, Morecambe was certainly a busy place, even in the early years of George V's reign.

Ship Inn, Musselburgh

108. MUSSELBURGH. From 1904 until 1928 electric trams were operated by the Musselburgh & District Electric Light and Traction Company Limited and ran to the east of Edinburgh along the coast from Joppa to Port Seton. We see here an open-top car by the Ship Inn. The line was much used by fish wives from Fisherrow who used to sell their fish in Edinburgh. Their baskets were carried on the front platform of the cars.

NEW BRIGHTON PIER.

109. NEW BRIGHTON. A fine view of an open-top car in its pale green livery to the left of the pier and amusement centre at this popular Wirral resort. The town is situated at the mouth of the Mersey, across the river from Liverpool and a little to the north of Birkenhead where, it will be recalled, the American George Francis Train had run his horse-drawn tram in 1860. The card was posted in August 1904.

The Wrench Series, No. 1255.

Newcastle (Staffs).

Nov. 6. 02.

I came up here on Monday. Yesterday went to a Chrys: Show at Hanley, it was lovely. Will write soon. ƒm.

High Street.

- Old Bank House - Newcastle.

110. NEWCASTLE-UNDER-LYME. A single-deck car in this Staffordshire city's High Street. The system was operated exclusively by over a hundred single-deck cars in the Potteries area, about which the novelist Arnold Bennett wrote so much. It lasted from the end of the last century until the late 1920's when it was replaced by buses. This undivided back card was printed in Saxony and posted in November 1902.

Central Station and Neville Street, *Newcastle-on-Tyne.*

111. NEWCASTLE-UPON-TYNE. Newcastle Corporation Tramways were one of the few authorities in the United Kingdom to begin operations with single-deck cars. The two shown here outside the city's Central Station in Neville Street were built in 1901. Double-deck open-top, balcony and enclosed cars were later added to the fleet which operated until March 1950, although some track continued to be used by Gateshead and District Tramways until August 1951.

Outside Newcastle United Football Ground after the Match.

112. NEWCASTLE-UPON-TYNE. Huge crowds emerge from Newcastle United Football Ground after a match, to be conveyed back to the city centre by a number of open-top cars. The crowd, which also contains a few females, certainly looks very orderly compared with some of those we encounter today! There seems to be just one policeman standing nonchalantly near the tram. This card forms an interesting comparison with No. 44, showing the crowds leaving a race meeting in Doncaster.

113. NEWPORT. A fine view of double-deck open car No. 38 at Stow Hill, which passes through the centre of this city in present-day Gwent. Electric cars began running here in the early 1900's, being abandoned in stages in 1930 and 1937. The system was self-contained, not linking up with any others in the area. The card is yet another example of the many which were printed in Germany prior to World War One.

Kettering Road, Northampton

Valentines Series   45632

114. NORTHAMPTON. This city's Corporation operated five short electric lines which ran from 1904 until the early 1930's. The majority of the cars was of the open-top type, although four single-deckers were added in the system's later years. In common with various other places in the area, the system was an isolated one. This card shows car No. 13 on its way along Kettering Road.

The Duck Pond, The Green, Norton-on-Tees. 155

115. NORTON. Posted in August 1914, this card shows an open-top car operated by Imperial Tramways Company Ltd. on the far side of the duck pond at the Green in this town situated to the north of Stockton-on-Tees. The system opened in May 1898 and was in 1921 split into companies operating in Middlesbrough and in Stockton and Thornaby. The latter part of the system closed in December 1931.

8 NORWICH. — *Royal Hotel and Prince of Wales Road.*

116. NORWICH. Three open-top cars in Prince of Wales Road are seen passing the imposing Royal Hotel. This city had electric cars from 1900 until 1935, their network covering just over fifteen miles. Note the attractive waiting shed with not a sign of vandalism.

NOTTINGHAM. GREAT MARKET PLACE.

117. NOTTINGHAM. The Corporation Tramways operated quite an extensive system which ran from 1901 until 1936. In this view of the Great Market Place, with a statue of Queen Victoria looking down on the scene, a number of cars, some open, others enclosed, can be seen skirting the market area with its host of stalls. It was probably a hot day, judging by the ladies with parasols.

Midland Station and Carrington Street, Nottingham

118. NOTTINGHAM. A balcony car in Carrington Street passes the Midland Station in the southern part of the city. This tram had originally been built with an open top, but was subsequently converted into a balcony car. It was quite common practice in Britain to modify early cars in this manner so that they fitted in better with later requirements. Note the horse bus on the left of the road.

119. NOTTINGHAM. This smartly dressed young lady about to enter this double-deck car could well have been recruited as a conductress or 'lady conductor' during World War One. It is, however, difficult to imagine that she would have had much in common with Annie, the conductress in D.H. Lawrence's story 'Tickets, Please', set in the Nottingham area. It is by no means uncommon today to find female drivers as well in many continental countries.

IMPROVING THE HIGH A PROPHETIC NIGHTMARE

120. OXFORD. A tram that never materialised! Horse trams operated in this university city from 1882 until the beginning of World War One. In 1906 there were plans to electrify and extend the network, but they never reached fruition. According to the writer of the card, posted in March 1906, there had been a small model of the intended electric tram exhibited in the city early in that same year.

Westgate and Midgate, Peterborough.

121. PETERBOROUGH. Open-top car No. 9 in Westgate and Midgate, in the centre of the city, on its way to Walton in the north-west. Peterborough had just over five miles of electric lines, and the system operated from January 1903 until November 1930. The car on the card, posted in April 1905, was built in 1902. The system had fourteen cars in all, but no car No. 13!

George Street, Plymouth

122. **PLYMOUTH.** Two open-top cars outside the Theatre Royal in George Street. The car on the right is for Peverell in the north of the city, very near Argyle football ground. Note the height of the conductor on the top of this car. Plymouth and Devonport had a complicated network of trams, most of which were replaced by buses between 1930 and 1939, although one route continued until 1945.

123. PORTSMOUTH. A decorated and illuminated balcony car of Portsmouth Corporation Tramways seen in a depot. The decorations were occasioned by a visit of the French fleet in 1905, hence the inscription 'Vive la France'. There was an extensive network of electric trams in and around Portsmouth operated by a number of different companies. They had the unusual gauge of 4 ft. 7¾ in. They were abandoned in 1936 in favour of trolleybuses.

124. RAMSGATE. Two of the open-top cars which used to run on the line to Margate via Broadstairs and St. Peters (cf. No. 105). The system was operated by the Isle of Thanet Electric Supply Company Limited. It was replaced by buses in 1937. The card is one of the 'Silverette' series started by Raphael Tuck & Sons in 1904.

125. READING. Two open-top cars in Broad Street in the centre of this Berkshire town. As can be seen, the street was true to its name, there being ample room between the trams for other vehicles, including the man with his hand cart. The car on the right is on its way to Caversham Bridge to the north of the city. Electric trams ran in and around Reading from 1903 until 1939. The card was posted in February 1908.

Esplanade, Rothesay.

126. ROTHESAY. One of the single-deck electric cars of the Rothesay Tramways Company Limited, which ran along the Esplanade of this Scottish port and resort, on the east coast of Bute island, from 1902 until 1936. Some of the cars used were of the open toastrack type, similar to those of Blackpool (cf. No. 20) and Southport (cf. No. 133). This is yet another example of a card printed in Germany prior to World War One.

127. SALFORD. An illuminated Salford car in a depot, decorated for the coronation of George V and Queen Mary in 1911. It was fairly common practice to decorate trams for special occasions or appeals (cf. Nos. 17, 70, 71 and 123). Salford Corporation Tramways operated electric cars from 1901 until 1947. The system therefore ceased two years before that of Manchester with which it shared some common track.

SCARBOROUGH - WESTBOROUGH

128. SCARBOROUGH. Open-top car No. 10, built in 1904, in the city's busy West-borough. This Yorkshire coastal resort had a fleet of about twenty-eight open-top cars, and the system operated from May 1904 until September 1931. There were also various cliff tramways and lifts near the city. This card was posted in August 1905.

TRAM JUNCTION, THE CRESCENT, SHEERNESS-ON-SEA.

129. SHEERNESS-ON-SEA. This undivided back card, posted in July 1903, shows open-top car No. 10 at the junction in the Crescent, well known for its clock tower. The system in this Kent resort had three routes, all of which started from the tower. The use of Siemens' bow collectors, just visible on the card, was a novel feature, as was the fact that it was the first complete system to be abandoned, this having taken place as early as 1917.

Fitzallan Square, Sheffield

Valentines Series

130. SHEFFIELD. Car No. 47, one of the single-deckers built in 1899, followed by an open-top double-decker, looking rather lonely amongst all the horse cabs in the city's Fitzallan Square. Several single-deck cars were used during the system's early years. Sheffield was the centre of a very extensive tramway network linking up with that of Rotherham, Mexborough and Barnsley. It ran from September 1899 until October 1960.

SHEFFIELD. MOORHEAD.

131. SHEFFIELD. Taken at Moorhead on a rainy day, this picture is of interest in that it shows both an open-top (No. 11) and an enclosed car (No. 154). The former was built in 1899, the latter in 1901, initially as an open-top car. The driver of No. 154 is wearing an oilskin to protect himself to some extent from the inclement weather. Note the elaborate pole supporting the overhead wires for the trams. The card was posted in April 1911.

BARGATE, SOUTHAMPTON.
TAKEN FROM ABOVE BAR

132. SOUTHAMPTON. The city had a large tramway network which was electrified in 1900 and continued to operate until 1949. Of special interest were the low-built double-deck cars designed to clear the mediaeval Bargate in High Street. Here car No. 6 is seen passing through this gate. It was eventually by-passed in 1938.

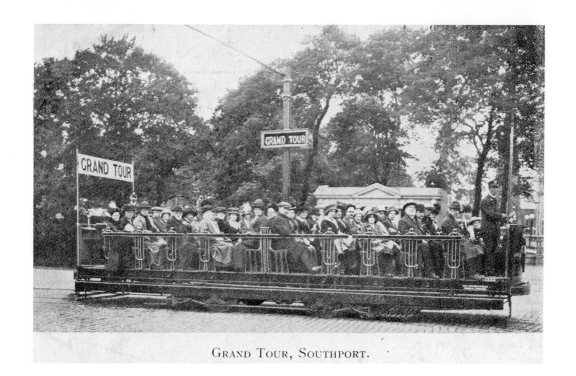

GRAND TOUR, SOUTHPORT.

133. SOUTHPORT. Forming a stark contrast to near-by Blackpool, this popular resort had a network of electric trams from the early 1900's until 1934. The car illustrated on this card, posted in September 1915, is of the completely open toastrack type, similar to that used for the circular tour in Blackpool (cf. No. 20). Its passengers nevertheless look much more dignified than those on the Blackpool car. Southport also had a pier tramway operated by cable.

134. SOUTHSEA. Electric trams, which were replaced by trolleybuses in 1936, connected this popular resort with Portsmouth (cf. No. 123). This charming card was posted in August 1907 and shows four open-top cars and a fine view of the Common which borders on the Esplanade and the sea. Note the many stalls set up on the Common and the caravan on the left.

TRAM ACCIDENT AT SOWERBY BRIDGE, OCT. 15th, 1907, (Three killed, many injured).

Lion Series

135. SOWERBY BRIDGE. A dramatic picture of an overturned car, resulting from an accident which took place on 15 October 1907 (a bad year for tram accidents, cf. Nos. 16 and 24). It is stated on the card that three people were killed and many injured, although the sender of the card adds that two more people subsequently died. This town in Yorkshire was served by Halifax trams (cf. Nos. 56 and 57).

HIGH STREET, SUNDERLAND.

136. SUNDERLAND. An open-top car in the High Street of this seaport at the mouth of the river Wear. This city had electric trams from August 1900 until September 1954. During the late 1940's some Manchester cars went to Sunderland while, in 1944, one Sunderland car went to Leeds. Such transfers were fairly common towards the end of various English systems, although very many cars were burnt.

137. SWANSEA. In addition to its own electric tramway system, the Swansea and Mumbles Railway ran around the edge of Swansea Bay to Mumbles pier. This line was operated by up to a dozen or more double-deck open-top tramway-type cars pulled by a steam locomotive. Part of such a unit is shown on this card, posted in January 1907. Electrification of the line finally took place in 1929, the last electric unit running in January 1960. There are however plans to restore at least part of the line.

FORE STREET & BURMESE MEMORIAL, TAUNTON.

E.T.W.D.

138. TAUNTON. The distinction of having the smallest urban electric tramway in Britain was enjoyed by this Somerset town with its one route $1\,^{2}/_{3}$ miles in length. It opened in August 1901 with six double-deck cars, one of which can be seen on this card, posted in October 1906. After ceasing operations temporarily, the line re-opened with single-deck cars, only to close finally in 1921. Car No. 2 is seen here in Fore Street about to pass the Burmese memorial.

Trainway Boulevard, Thorpe Bay

139. THORPE BAY. The single-deck car shown on this card was of the cross-bench seating type, built in 1914. The section along the Southchurch and Thorpe Bay boulevards was on reserved track and constructed in 1913-14. Southend-on-Sea Corporation Light Railways, which ran electric cars from July 1901 until April 1942, served this resort.

22412
SIX CHIMNEYS, KIRKGATE, WAKEFIELD.

140. WAKEFIELD. An open-top car in Kirkgate. As in Lancashire and North Cheshire, there was a closely-knit network of trams in the former West Riding of Yorkshire, this also involving Wakefield, where the main routes were abandoned in 1932. Note the fine timbered houses, the ground floors of which are occupied by an antique dealer. The card was published by Boots Cash Chemist's.

141. WAKEFIELD. Trams were less deterred or affected by adverse weather conditions, such as fog and snow, than many other types of road transport. Despite their superiority, even they had their limitations, as shown by these two Wakefield open-top cars stranded in a snowdrift in Horbury Road, on the route from Wakefield to Horbury, in the direction of Dewsbury.

CHURCH STREET.

WEST HARTLEPOOL.

3587

Dear Chrissie

Come down to night. Ma not well

142. WEST HARTLEPOOL. An open-top car of West Hartlepool Corporation Tramways in the city's Church Street. This line, previously operated by steam trams, was electrified as early as 1896. It is of interest that all this system's double-deck cars were of the open-top type. It closed in March 1927. The message on the front of this undivided back card, posted in October 1902, is revealing, i.e. 'Come down tonight. Ma not well.'

Weston-super-Mare Grand Pier & Pavilion.
L.B.W. 19.
First Section opened June 11th 1904.

143. WESTON-SUPER-MARE. Resembling a continental 'Gruss aus' card, this picture shows an open-top and a single-deck toastrack car passing the entrance to this Somerset resort's grand pier and pavilion. Weston-super-Mare kept its trams until 1937 when they were replaced by Bristol buses, although the company continued to supply electricity until 1948. This attractive card was posted in July 1905.

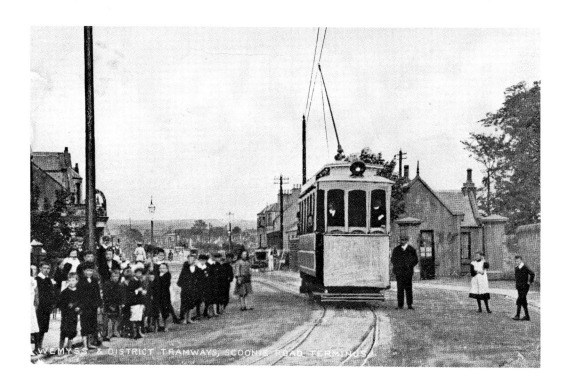

144. WEMYSS. The Wemyss & District Tramway Co. Ltd. operated electric cars from August 1906 until January 1932 from Gallatown to Leven, via Wemyss and Methil. All the trams of this Scottish system were single-deckers with clerestory roofs, being typically American rather than British in appearance. This card, posted in Leven in August 1916, shows one of these cars at Scoone Road terminus.

Oxley Bank. (Tram terminus.)

145. **WOLVERHAMPTON.** Posted in July 1910, this card shows open-top car No. 14 at the Oxley Bank terminus, to the north-west of this Midlands town. There was a complicated system of ownership of the various lines in this part of the country with much through running of services based on Wolverhampton, Walsall, Dudley, Stourbridge and Birmingham. Wolverhampton's own trams were replaced by trolleybuses in the late 1920's.

Worcester Electric Tramway Siege, 1903-4.

"what's it coming to? Ichabod!!

T. Bennett & Sons, Photographers,
Worcester and Malvern.

146. WORCESTER. Tracklaying work during 1903 and 1904 in Worcester's city centre. Prior to electric trams the city had a horse-drawn system from 1882 until 1903. The electric system serving the city and its environs was replaced by buses in 1928. The card, posted in March 1904 to an address in Sydney, Australia, obviously represented something highly undesirable to its writer with his exclamation 'Ichabod!!'

147. YORK. An early Edwardian card shows an open-top horse-drawn tram crossing the bridge over the Ouse. Note the back-to-back seating arrangement on the top deck. It was not until 1910 that York's horse-drawn trams were replaced by municipal electric tramways. These latter were abandoned in 1935. Also on the bridge is an enclosed single-deck horse bus.

THE HILLY BIT OF OLD YORK

148. YORK. Posted in September 1906, this comic card is of the same type as that of Cambridge (cf. No. 31). There is a stark contrast between the three emaciated horses and the well-fed driver. The drawing emphasizes one of the main disadvantages of horse-drawn trams, i.e. their difficulty in coping easily with steep terrains.

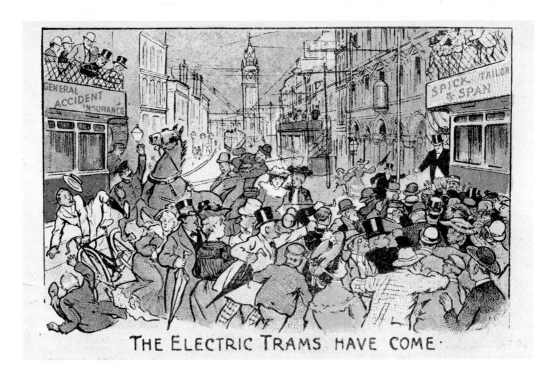

THE ELECTRIC TRAMS HAVE COME·

149. This early Edwardian comic card, posted in Belfast in August 1905, was intended to draw attention to the havoc caused to horse-drawn vehicles and other road-users by the advent of electric trams. There had, of course, been similar reactions to early motor cars. With the passage of time the advantages of electric trams were however found to be far in excess of their disadvantages.

THE POLICEMAN SAID "FOLLOW THE TRAM-LINES."

150. The caption on this comic card, drawn by Dudley Buxton, who worked for various publishers in the early years of the century, i.e. 'The policeman said 'Follow the tram-lines'' is still good advice which I have occasionally given to people wanting to walk to a specific destination. Note the metathesis in the name of the brand of pickles on the front of the first tram, i.e. 'Boss and Crackwells' for 'Cross and Blackwells'.